Write Your Family Story:
Leaving a Living Legacy

By Judy H. Wright

aka Auntie Artichoke

Write Your Family Story: Leaving a Living Legacy

© 2012 by Judy H. Wright, Family Educator and Author in Residence at
Artichoke Press
2400 West Central, Missoula MT 59801

Web site: www.ArtichokePress.com

Parenting Blog: www.AskAuntieArtichoke.com

For additional parenting, wellness, life-story writing, end-of-life books and programs please see our website or contact us directly.

All rights reserved. No part of this publication may be reproduced, stored in a retrieval system, or transmitted in any form or by any means without prior written permission from the publisher.

ISBN-13: 978-1481286312
ISBN-10: 1481286315

Self-published in the United States of America by:

ARTICHOKE PRESS LLC

Medical Disclaimer: Please use this book as a guide and suggestions, not as medical or psychological advice. Judy H. Wright is not a doctor, licensed counselor or professional consultant. She is a parent educator and family advocate. If you are concerned about some aspect of your child's development, or your own mental health, do not hesitate to seek professional help.

Affiliate Disclaimer: Some of the resources and programs that are recommended in this eBook pay a small commission to the author when you buy them. This commission is used to further the goals of those who protect children, so we appreciate your support. You pay the same amount, but the company pays Artichoke Press for the referral.

. Dedicated to the hundreds of life story class members
who have attended my writing classes.

Your stories are incredible and so are you

Write Your Family Story: Leaving a Living Legacy	7
Why Write a Memoir?	7
Genealogy is Facts	7
Life Narratives Help You Relate	8
Life Stories Keep Going	9
You Will Never Regret Writing Something, No Matter How Small	12
Today is the day to do it	12
Methods of Memoir Making	14
Address books and phone logs	14
Advanced Directives	15
Anecdotes	15
Anthology	15
Autobiography	16
Baby Books	16
Biography	17
Blueprints	18
Calendars or Day Timers	19
Caregiver's Notes and Reflections	20
Christmas Letters	20
Company or Family Newsletters	21
Cookbooks and Recipe Files	22
CYA files	23
Diary	23
Descriptions	24
Essays	24
E-mail or E-zine	25
Ethical Will or Ethical Letter	25
Eulogies	26
Family Record	27
Fill-in- the-Blank-Books	27
Just Do It.	28
Funeral Programs	28
Genealogy	29
Guest Books	30
Interview	30
Jokes and cartoons	32
Journals	32
Last Will and Testament	33

Legal Records	33
Letters	34
Life Events	35
Lists, lists and more lists	35
Medical Records	36
Memoirs	37
Message in a bottle	37
Newspapers and magazines	38
Obituary	38
Parable	40
Photo scribing	40
Postcards	41
Resumes	41
School Records and Papers	42
Scrap booking:	43
Stories	44
Tales and Fables	44
Tributes	45

Reasons for Recording Your Life Story 48
Write Your Slice of Life - 6 Easy Steps 51
    1. *Be brief.* *51*
    2. *Tell a story.* *51*
    3. *Make a point.* *51*
    4. *Use your senses.* *52*
    5. *Tell about the ordinary.* *52*
    6. *Make it engaging.* *52*

About The Author 54
Resources for Parents, Teachers and other Caring Adults 56

Write Your Family Story: Leaving a Living Legacy

Why Write a Memoir?

All over the world people are eager and anxious to learn about their family heritage. However, as a trained parent and life educator, I have found that modern families are in many times complicated, isolated and confused about their roots.

People everywhere, feel some of the emptiness in their life when talking about close family relationships. They hunger for morsels of information that will tell them about who they are and why they do what they do. They look to the past for information about their life and the future of their children.

Millions of parents, children, aunts, uncles, cousins, nephew, nieces, in-laws, out-laws, maternal and paternal grandparents, and step-parents and step-siblings are scattered by area and conflicted stories.

Genealogy is Facts

Many people enjoy doing the puzzle of a family tree. They enjoy studying a long list of names, places and events that are connected through family ties.

For some the names and dates are enough to prove that they come from a long line of people. It was never enough for me. I wanted to know them as individuals and to hear their stories.

When I tried to do genealogy I became frustrated, annoyed and overwhelmed. Sure you can find the date of birth, marriage and death, but I needed the stories in between.

Would you rather do a genealogy study or write a few of your personal memoirs? Your decedents can find the names and numbers online. But only you know the stories.

Each of us has a unique history to draw on to tell our life story. We can also select the method, the reason and how much we want to reveal of the personal knowledge and information that we alone possess.

Life Narratives Help You Relate

Most people have some knowledge of at least two generations back. Even just writing down a few of the memories of stories you heard as a child will help the reader to relate to the ancestor as a person, rather than a date and burial place.

Written words are a special heirloom. Captured in tangible form, a life story becomes a permanent, priceless memento of your family's heritage. It is a document that honors all your loved ones- both the storyteller and story readers for generations to come.

A life story is anything that describes a period in someone's life. It can cover a space of time as short as the few minutes it took to rope that first steer or as long as the tale from diaper days to twilight years. It can also be a compilation of anecdotes, stories, experiences, memories, journal entries, or captions on snap shots.

Like the artichoke, which we have chosen as our logo, you need to peel off many layers to get to the heart of the story. Underneath all those leaves with sharp, prickly ends you will find an essential truth. The truth of the story is that which speaks to your heart and touches you in a way that nothing else could.

Life Stories Keep Going

I firmly believe that each of us has a destiny and purpose in this life and we have wisdom to share.

Most of us have no idea how extensive an impact we have made on the lives of others we come across in our daily life. By exploring some of your own accomplishments or failures, pleasures and pains, lessons learned easily as well as with great sorrow, you will share your wisdom and humanity with readers.

As you reflect on your story, you will come to recognize the different crossroads through each phase of your life. While you and you alone can choose what to include, know that readers are not going to judge you nearly as hard as you have. They will be relieved to find out that life was not always easy and you were not always smart.

A life story is an on-going process that continues beyond your lifetime. When someone reads or glances at this written legacy, the subject of the story comes to life again. Your words can warm, inspire, instruct, or encourage the reader as they think of you and your experiences, or the experiences of the person you are writing about.

Many people have been prompted, both by their own spirits and the voices of others, to record highlights of their lives.

You may be unsure of how and when to begin. The task can seem daunting, but the effort will be very worthwhile. Everyone for generations to come will be grateful you were willing to sacrifice other easier pursuits in order to write those memoirs or leave a paper trail of who you are, where you have been, and what you believed. It is the same whether you do this for your own life or gather the information to record the life story of someone you know.

The most important step in compiling memoirs is that you do something NOW. Write down the story, joke, recipe, instructions or anecdotes that you have been meaning to for so long. There is no such thing as too little or too much. There is no good writing or bad writing. There is no such thing as "not important enough."

In the experience of writing a life story, you will find the introspection, learning process and absolute joy of reminiscing to be therapeutic and healing. You can capture the feelings and emotions of a particular time or experience. You can add to it later. Or you can do a whole autobiography or biography later in life.

But begin today to capture the essence of the vital life you are writing about, and the world of that person's experiences.

You Will Never Regret Writing Something, No Matter How Small

Never has there been an author who wishes they would not have done the book, story or manuscript. If a noted publisher grabs it and it gets made into a movie to be seen by thousands, that will be great. If, on the other hand, no one else ever reads it, you will still find the self-introspection, learning process and absolute joy of reminiscing to be very therapeutic and healing.

You can capture the feelings and emotions of a particular time or experience, then add to it next year or do a whole autobiography when you retire.

But begin TODAY to capture the essence of who you are and the lessons you have to teach. You will find this a reoccurring theme in life stories.

Today is the day to do it.

The following list describes various methods for capturing a moment in time. You will probably use a combination of these methods and indeed, may be surprised to see how many you already have in your possession.

They are listed in alphabetical order, not in order of importance, ease of doing, or even most interesting.

All written accounts are important, interesting and easy to do once you realize that you are giving your many readers clues about your life.

You are peeling down the leaves on the artichoke of life, with its layers of daily activities, major and minor adversities, joyful activities, lessons learned and messages taught.

Those who are privileged to reach the heart will love you even more. They will be encouraged to keep going and perhaps even inspired by your words. But the main emotion will be one of gratitude that you made the effort to share your wisdom in some small way.

So gather your little bits and pieces from here and there, put them in a timeline, or chronological order.

You may want to check our website http://www.MontanaStoryKeepers for a great organizational tool that assists in building a timeline, which is the foundation of all life stories.

Once you are organized, the stories will just flow. Write them just as you remember, you can worry about spelling later. Have fun.

Methods of Memoir Making

There are hundreds of different ways to make your stamp on life. No matter whether it is writing on the back of photos or a long detailed autobiography, it is enough.

I hope you enjoy reading these various definitions and recognizing that you already are doing some memoir making.

Address books and phone logs

This is a very important part of the paper trail used in compiling a narrative of yourself or someone else. Whose name is recorded and why? Which names have notes written by them? Does this record list best friends, church members, distant cousins, doctors, dentists and important business contacts? Can you gain a more rounded view of the person by seeing who they thought was important enough to maintain contact with on a consistent basis?

Advanced Directives

Other names for these documents that may be more familiar are *living wills* or *durable powers of attorney for health care*. Written when the person is in good health and of sound mind, these legal papers indicate the wishes in regard to issues which might come up when and if the writer is not in a position to make decisions for him/herself.

While usually not long and involved, many people make very specific statements or requests, which leave a witness to the philosophy and beliefs of the writer.

Anecdotes

These are short accounts of interesting, often biographical, incidents. Gather your anecdotes, throw in a few pages of dialogue or commentary to bridge from one story to the next and you have a wonderful life story.

Good examples of anecdotes are found in Reader's Digest or Chicken Soup for the Soul. Two or three page stories that contain a beginning, middle and an end. It needs a hook to hold the interest of the reader, a theme that runs through it, and a conclusion that teaches or tells the reader something.

Anthology

Another name for an anthology is a collection of writings. Perhaps you may find a notebook full of poetry and prose your grandmother wrote, or you may just keep random written notes on a specific subject or related subjects scattered throughout your house, car, dresser and journal. Collected together and indexed they become an anthology.

Autobiography

This is the complete account of a whole life, usually in chronological order. An autobiography is based on fact, research and history. It is possible to have your autobiography ghost-written, which means someone else writes your story from your point of view. When you use a ghostwriter, you retain authorship. The best autobiographies are rich in scenes and details, utilizing the reader's senses to bring them fully into the story. When writing an autobiography the reader wants to know what you had for breakfast, but not every day!

Baby Books

The record will only be complete and in pristine shape after the first child unless you are the Queen Mother and have servants who can help. But even those baby books with just a few notations are keepsakes. Now is a good time to fill in the gaps by writing down interesting childhood incidents before you forget.

Why not ask one of the grandparents to remember and record the stories of when the children were young. They come from a different perspective and think the children were absolutely brilliant when the little darlings dialed Africa on the phone or put Cheerios up their noses.

Authors note: I was very grateful and touched to be able to read from our daughter Bethany's baby book at her wedding. Everyone had tears in their eyes as we shared the thoughts, feelings and hopes for her as recorded twenty years earlier at her birth.

Biography

This tome of information is accomplished when someone writes a life story other than their own and they retain authorship. If you pay them to do it, it is called a *commissioned biography*, and you have some control over the finished product. There are also unauthorized biographies where the subject (usually someone famous) is either dead, never consulted or refuses to give permission. The information for such a biography is then gained from news articles and interviews with friends, enemies and the milkman.

Blueprints

Most people remember in pictures and scenes. Nothing stirs the memory like a photo or drawing of a childhood home.

Sketching a floor plan or looking at the actual architectural drawing, will bring hidden remembrances of places, people, sounds, smells, emotions as if you had been there just yesterday.

Be sure to sketch or remember the outbuildings, trees and lawn. Much of our most pleasurable childhood took place outside playing with siblings, cousins or friends.

It is also helpful for the reader to be able to anchor in their imagination the scene of your stories. When you draw out the floor plan, you can walk the reader through the house, apartment or farm.

Author's note: I have used this technique in working with trauma victims and asked them to draw a safe place in their childhood. The instructions are to draw what you would see if you were in a plane hovering over the scene.

This has been very therapeutic as they recognized the "safe place" of childhood has often been recreated in some form of adult life.

One woman broke down in tears when she realized that both she and her brother had bought or built homes that resembled the floor plan of their grandparent's home. It had been a haven of security for them as children.

Calendars or Day Timers

It is amazing the snapshot of daily life that can be obtained from keeping a yearly appointment calendar. The notes and comments can then be expanded into a longer narrative of those subjects, which hold special meaning.

Many people use their calendar to make a timeline of the year, which highlights the special times of each month.

Authors note: A family calendar may have something as innocuous as "soccer game-State". But when you see the note, it jogs your memory into the feelings, emotions and jubilation you had when your son scored the winning goal.

You can then take those memories and write a short essay about that time. Be sure to ask your son what he remembers about the event.

Caregiver's Notes and Reflections

As our population grows older, there may be less time spent with family and more spent with caregivers. A communication log or ongoing journal left on a handy bedside table makes it easy for all visitors, family and caregivers to record notes, observations and comments.

This communication log not only records changes in health, diet or medication but also is a wonderful spot to record the stories and experiences of the patient.

Frequently the most profound and meaningful conversations come at unexpected times. By sharing the gist of the conversations or requests with the family, with permission of the patient of course, the transitions and traumas of an illness are lessened.

The family, caregiver and patient are then able to form a circle of love and concern that is more inclusive of the full picture.

Christmas Letters

I know, I know, some people hate them, but Christmas or holiday letters do provide a chance to reflect and recount your many blessings, family activities and events on a yearly basis. By saving annual letters, you will have a record of the transitions in your family life.

Vera Rosenbluth, a personal historian friend from Vancouver, BC shared with the APH list some she had heard on the CBC radio program "Wasted Words". The program asked for people to come up with words which have not yet been invented for "the form letter families send out around Christmas time to boast about their travels, social triumphs and career accomplishments." The suggested words were: conceitsheet, brage carta, brag rag, better-letter, boast-it-note, borrespondence, bragalougue, bragitorial, famail, famspam, gloatnote etc.

I still love them, so keep them coming.

Company or Family Newsletters

This venue of information sharing is more and more common as a means of communication. Companies are finding that articles of interest, photos of employees and their stories and a listing of upcoming events are very effective methods of creating "ownership".

Family newsletters may be written by one relative after gathering information and then mailed to members of the immediate and extended family. Another popular method is to create a 'round robin', which means that as people on the mailing list receive the envelope with letters; they add their own news, and send it on.

Cookbooks and Recipe Files

Nothing can bring memories back like the taste, smell and texture of a cookie baked from an old family recipe. Aside from the treasure of cookbooks are the asides that many cooks add to the page; "this was good, but Ralph likes more nuts, remember that for next time" or "served this for Emily's wedding and got so many compliments."

Another option is to write down a family recipe and then do a small story concerning how, when and where the dish was served.

Do a bit of family history surrounding food, utilizing the five senses of taste, smell, hear, touch and sight. Make the reader hungry!

I remember hearing an elderly woman in one of my classes say that if there was ever a famine in the land, they could boil her cookbook and make soup; it had so many splatters on it from when she was cooking.

CYA files

These are files and memos created during times of great stress often related to business.

Author's note; Quite frankly, a CYA (cover your fanny) file had not occurred to me until a retired executive in a writing class said that he was caught in the middle of a hostile takeover and wasn't sure from day to day whether he would have a job or who he could trust. He developed a file, which he kept at home, of all the events, players, strategies and feelings about what was transpiring on a daily and weekly basis. Several years later he used that file to recreate that stressful period in his life, come to grip with some of the decisions he made and to look at the painful experience with more compassionate eyes.

Diary

This is a daily record of the trivial threads that make up your life. Taken as a whole, diaries are a wonderful rich tapestry that gives an overview as well as details that are too easily forgotten.

Historians and families are forever grateful to those diligent men and women who took time to record on a regular basis the goings and comings of their world.

No matter how many times I swear that I will write in my diary and exercise daily, I usually don't. But the times I do, I feel better about myself. So I will buy another one next year and swear again to write in it daily, if even just to record my gratitude list.

Descriptions

Sometimes you will find that while Aunt Mary is deaf, cranky and unwilling to tell you her life story, she may be willing to describe a dress she had as a young girl, what the family farmhouse looked like or even how Uncle Frank looked.

Write it down. The more details, the more vivid the picture. A description in a letter from a brother serving in the Korean War of the set of china he had sent his mother helped the family find it among the boxes stored in the attic and made a wonderful family story.

Essays

This is a short non-fiction piece on a particular subject or theme that tries to make a point in an interesting way. When it concerns you and your point of view, it is called a personal essay. Many times essays are required in English classes to assist students in organizing thoughts and coming to a logical conclusion.

Even though you hated writing "What I did on my summer vacation" as a ten year old, those few paragraphs make fascinating reading now. When cleaning the attic or garage don't throw out the old school papers, they give a brief view of the life of the writer.

E-mail or E-zine

E-zine or net-zines are newsletters written on the net. While this is the easiest, fastest and cheapest method of communicating by the written word available today, there is a certain "netiquette" that should be followed. For example: avoid the use of all capital letters, it comes across as anger.

When communicating in e-mail don't hit delete after sending a reply, but rather store the correspondence in a folder. These will someday have the same value to your children's children as the handwritten letters between your ancestors.

Ethical Will or Ethical Letter

This was a medieval practice in the 11th or 12th centuries, mainly in the Hebrew culture but also in some Muslim and Christian faiths.

It is essentially a legacy and listing of spiritual values and ethical practices that differ from material possessions.

Traditionally a rabbi or patriarch wrote the letter for his children or the faith community as a whole.

The ethical will was typically shared at the death of the writer. It may include a summary of the individual's values and standards as well as burial and mourning wishes. Ethical letters were shared when people were separated by distance or time.

The goal of an ethical letter is to communicate life lessons and impart wisdom to children, grandchildren and others who might wish to emulate your standards.

Today many Hospice organizations encourage patients who are facing life's end to write ethical letters to their family.

Eulogies

This is an opportunity to pay homage to a person who has passed away as well as express the sorrow at his or her passing. Traditionally its function was to awaken tears among the mourners.

The eulogy usually takes the obituary or death notice a step further and gives more depth and insight into the deceased. Many contain funny stories or anecdotes that help the mourners remember the personality and characteristics of their loved one.

This oration of high praise is usually written down, of only in notes for the speaker. Do not allow this record to be consigned to a suit pocket or the wastebasket. It contains the highlights of a person's life and thus should be kept with other important papers.

Family Record

This is not as official as a genealogical record and may be kept in the front of a family bible or a separate book that details the history of the family. It may include a limited or a lot of information on a number of different subjects, depending on the space used and the diligence of the writer. To have a family history written by the hand of an ancestor is a priceless heirloom

Author's Note: Don't worry if your writing efforts will be good enough. Keep in mind that the Ark was built as a family project, while the Titanic was designed and built by professionals.

Fill-in- the-Blank-Books

These little expensive books are available for every conceivable connection; grandmothers, grandfathers, mothers, fathers, sisters, brothers, godparents, teachers, neighbors etc. Lots of people purchase them for gifts.

Makes me wish I had published them!

Very few gift receivers utilize them, however, because they may be intimidated or think they have to finish them in order for them to have value.

The true value of these books is the memory joggers and the questions, which assist the writer to get started. Even if you only fill in a few of the blanks, you will have left a written snippet of your life.

You can download a perfectly lovely one for free at www.igrandparents.com.

If you worry about who in the family will receive the actual book, just use the questions as a springboard for your own life story written on regular paper and thus easily copied.

Just Do It.

Your family will be so grateful and they can fight over who gets the gravy ladle or the patchwork quilt.

Funeral Programs

These can become true family keepsakes if a little time and thought is put into the preparation. You **do not** have to use the pre-printed forms that funeral homes sell you. Many people include a short life sketch, photo and names of descendants.

Author's note: In my mother's funeral program we included a collage of photos of her, recipes that were well-loved and a poem she had written. This was in addition to the life sketch and program of the service. It was a keepsake for those who attended and a wonderful remembrance when sent to those who could not attend.

Genealogy

This refers to detailed information about your family and ancestors on your individual family tree. This study will usually go back through many generations over several centuries and could involve records in various countries and languages.

It involves a lot of research and documentation to get names and dates and places spelled and listed correctly.

Not only does this important work look at family lineage but also at the social history. It can assist you to place your loved ones in the proper time and space in history.

Author's Note: I am grateful God created those diligent people who can spend hours and hours and hours poring over old records to find a single date. I will buy their books and shake their hands at a family reunion, but will never have the patience to do genealogy.

Guest Books

Who's who in the world of family reunions or parties? Who visited the cabin in the mountains? Who came to the funeral for Grandma? Why were they willing to travel long distances and at a great expense in order to show their respect for her and comfort the family? What is the story?

Author's note: We keep a guest book near our front door and ask guests (when we remember) to sign the book and leave us a blessing. Those blessings from friends and family are priceless. Looking at the guest book from our wedding nearly 40 years ago, I can still picture family and friends, many of whom I have not seen since then.

Interview

You may want to be interviewed or you may want to interview others in order to assist them in recording their life stories.

It may be a formal question-and-answer session by a journalist. In that case they retain the right of editing and publishing their version in a magazine or newspaper. The storyteller rarely gets to preview the piece before it is published.

Interviews by personal or oral historians are different because the story is yours, and they are the conduit or method of getting the story down. It is easier from someone other than family to interview a loved one. They are hearing the story with fresh ears and know how to probe to get the "rest of the story."

You will be given the opportunity to proof the pieces, make changes or additions. The finished product belongs to you and your heirs.

Informal interviews can range from a conversation with grandparents to a taped and guided dialogue with a listener who will transcribe the tapes for a written history or leave in audio form for an oral history.

Jokes and cartoons

Did your dad send you a funny card for your birthday? Does your grandma clip cartoons and put them on the fridge? Do you get jokes in your e-mail from a favorite uncle? Not only do the jokes and cartoons bring a smile to your face, so does the memory of who sent them and why he/she thought that particular one was funny.

He: Hey honey, what do you call a memoir of someone who idolizes a talk show host?

She: I give up, what?
He:" The Fan Tome of The Oprah!"

Journals

A journal is wide open as far as what form and substance it takes. It is usually a record of a specific time, project or interest. It can be a daily recording of experiences and observations or it can be written in occasionally to capture feelings and facts concerning an important aspect of daily lives.

Many people who are not disciplined or moved to keep a diary will find time to record thoughts in a journal about a trip, spiritual journeys, parenting, work, dreams, prayers, or the quality of life.

Many people find that keeping a journal is a very healing exercise. When they write about heartbreak, a joy, or simply put confusing thoughts on paper in an effort to make some sort of sense, they are writing to heal themselves - emotionally, spiritually and sometimes physically.

When you have access to a journal of an ancestor, you have access to their heart.

Last Will and Testament

This legal document lists assets, property and tangible goods and how they are to be disbursed. Most will name an executor or trustee of the will who sees that the wishes of the deceased are carried out.

It is not unusual to have a written letter which goes along with the legal papers describing last wishes and information that the deceased wishes to be shared after his or her demise. This can either be an ethical will or simply a letter of instructions.

Legal Records

Legal records can be a goldmine of information about your family. The dates, events, names, places, and activities of ancestors can be traced by looking at legal records.

With the advent of computers and the Internet, it is possible to find records that are thousands of miles away. Genealogists have said that looking in old records is much like searching for the missing piece in a 10,000 piece jigsaw puzzle; you find one clue which leads you to another clue, etc.

Letters

Many memoirs, autobiographies and biographies would not be here today if it were not for boxes of old letters hidden in the back of a closet or bottom of an old trunk. Most of these letters are thoughtful outpouring of feelings and enough 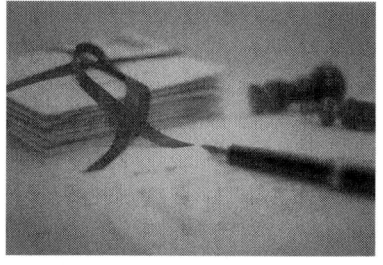 detail that the reader can see in his mind's eye what the writer is describing.

Authors note: A real life example is Jessie Dombey, who wrote daily letters to her daughter who was stationed overseas with the WAC's during the Korean conflict. The letters, written in poetry and illustrated by Jessie, told of life at home on the Montana ranch: what cows were calving, what cowboys were learning to dance, what was served for dinner, and other general information. They were so loved that after Ione had read them, she posted them to a bulletin board for all the company to share. Members of the company would write Jesse asking to hear more about certain cowboys or to know the rest of the story concerning a sick horse. They were later made into a book entitled "Letters to a WAC."

Life Events

Your pride, excitement and emotion over a recognized life event, accomplishment, or rite of passage is a part of your history and therefore worth preserving. For example: childbirth, marriage, illness of yourself or family member, new home, job etc.

It is much more interesting when you are able to write about your feelings surrounding an event rather than just recording the event.

Typically, our lives tend to run in seven-year cycles and dividing the years as such makes it easy to remember and place life events in the correct chorological order. This really helps to anchor time and event in our minds.

A great way to define different periods is by using house addresses, cars owned, jobs held, talents developed, energy cycles, pets, etc. Our lives are segmented more by the events that happen than the years on the calendar.

Lists, lists and more lists

Make a list of old toys, places you have lived, places you have worked, books you have read, plays you have seen, food that you love, favorite fishing holes, people who came to your wedding, people you play cards with, old neighbors, classmates, teachers, cars you have owned, family pets, things that bug you, things that make you happy, and spiritual experiences.

On the top of a blank piece of paper put "I remember my mother (or father, house, school etc) and then just do automatic writing of short phrases consisting of three to five words for at least ten minutes.

You will be amazed at the number of insightful memory joggers that fill the page. You may want to circle some of them and expand them into a story.

If, every time you had a few minutes while waiting for an appointment, the kids to finish practice, or a real person to come on line, you jotted down a different list, you would have the basis for a complete memoir.

Medical Records

Studies validate use of family health history as gold standard in disease risk assessment. Family health history assessment is an inexpensive, simple and effective tool to help access personal disease risks.

There is a free tool available at www.talkhealthhistory.org You will want to ask to have it kept with your medical records.

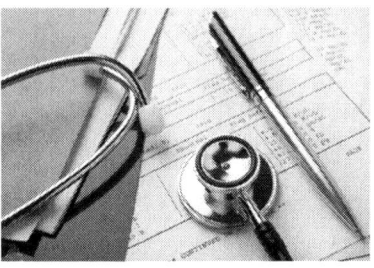

These records are yours and you may request a copy of them. These are invaluable documents if you want to build a gen-o-gram or medical family tree for your descendants.

Memoirs

This is a record of events based on your observations. They may include special events, incidents, experiences, achievements and feelings. You may choose this method to write about a certain period in your life or perhaps a sequence of events that helped you to form your philosophy of life.

Some people have likened a memoir to single scenes in a movie or "a slice of life" or even a select part of a longer autobiography.

Just as I used the analogy of an autobiography to a strand of pearls, I think of memoirs or personal essays as individual pearls which could stand alone or be gathered in shorter version of a bracelet or chocker necklace.

Message in a bottle

This one was just thrown in to see how many people really read this whole book. If you do have a message in a bottle story or you read the entire book write me at judy@artichokepresss.com and I will send you a free report on "What is truth?" Or as in the case of most families, whose truth is truer?

Newspapers and magazines

Have you ever been in print? Have you ever written a letter to the editor, been quoted in an article or mentioned in an industry newsletter? These little tidbits are part of your paper trail.

Obituary

People often do not realize that there are two ways to announce a person's death - a death notice, which is a paid listing in a newspaper, and an obituary, which is a news story.

Families purchase death notices and obituaries and they are free to say whatever they wish as long as it is appropriate in length and taste.

Most are submitted by the funeral home and are written from information gathered on a form filled out by the family.

If you are smart, you will write your own and keep it with your advanced directives. Family members often don't know what was important for you and are trying to come up with dates and names under a great deal of pressure and stress.

Authors Note: It makes me crazy when I read an obituary about a strong, vital, involved and talented woman written by a grieving son. Almost always it talks about what a good cook she was and how her cinnamon rolls could melt in your mouth. Because that was the context where he knew her best, it is what is focused on. However, those of us who worked beside her on boards and committees knew that she had so many other qualities that could have been celebrated. Write your own. I have. I have also planned the songs,

speakers and refreshments served after the service.

However, if the deceased was a prominent citizen the newspaper may choose to run their own obituary, which will be considered news and the family has little control over what is printed.

Most media have obituaries on file for prominent people and simply update it at the time of death.

It may list the cause of death or the circumstances as well as other interesting aspects of a person's life if it would be of interest to the reading public.

Death notices and obituaries are wonderful sources of information in writing life stories.

Parable

This is a short allegorical story designed to teach some moral truth or lesson. Many families have traditional stories that are used in teaching moments when lectures won't work.

If you are looking for a good collection of these stories, check out William J Bennett's "The Book of Virtues- A Treasury of Great Moral Stories."

The hope is that the listener or reader will see a parallel to their own life situation and draw logical conclusions.

If not, you may have to point out that when great grandpa lost his business during the depression, he started over again.

This will encourage the soccer player to recognize that every life has some wins and some losses.

Photo scribing

Denis Ledoux, who wrote a book by the same name, has made this method popular. It actually is an expanded photo album, which highlights the best photograph of a particular time or event.

This requires going through the boxes and drawers of snapshots and pictures and selecting those that have special meaning. You then write a short paragraph or cameo narrative that tells the story behind the photo or fills the gap between the pictures.

The hardest part of this venue is throwing away the other 345 pictures of the family standing in front of Old Faithful.

Postcards

Anyone who has ever visited the Charlie Russell Museum in Great Falls, Montana, would understand the power of a history written and illustrated on post cards. These small rectangular messages can give a bird's eye view of daily life and travel.

Authors Note: Jessie Dombey, mentioned above, shared a box of postcards she and her sister had exchanged when she was pregnant with her first child and thousands of miles away from home and loved ones. Written in the early 1900's they cost a penny to mail and arrived at her home about a week after they had been sent. Not only did they encourage and cheer the young bride, but made suggestions for names for the new baby. The child was named lone, which was the suggestion that arrived the same day the baby did.

Resumes

Anyone who has spent time in Corporate America has at least four or five of these. If you have not developed one you should. It is a good way to recognize your own successes and to realize all that you have accomplished.

Keep it with your obituary, so the kids will know some of your professional accomplishments in addition to making cinnamon rolls.

School Records and Papers

Build a treasure box for each of your children by covering an apple box with Contac paper. They can store their precious papers there.

One mother I know allows the children to put their best and most important paper and a current picture in their backpack at the end of the school year. She writes the year on the pack and stores it in the garage on a high shelf.

In September they get a new backpack and know that it will be the repository at the end of the school year.

Authors note: Just thinking about it makes me feel weepy and nostalgic; I imagine that her husband felt irritated and annoyed that there were shelves full of old backpacks in the garage. He'll be glad to read them someday and so will the children when they have children.

Scrap booking:

Scrap booking stores and websites are popping up all over. This is becoming a very popular pastime and classes are held teaching how to add borders, stickers and other features which make each page a study in creativity.

Most pages will have a short narrative by each item explaining the item or photo.

Each scrapbook tends to hold a collection of memories, photos and mementos from a period in your life or of a specific person. Most scrapbooks seem to focus on one theme or person.

Stories

Ahhhhh, this is the golden treasure of all life narratives. This is the one that bridges the generations and holds us together with tradition, tales and anecdotes.

Lucky is the family which has its stories recorded. In order to have life in your life story or memoir, you must have the stories.

Build the scenes and characters by using who, what, where, when, why and how and your story will have the drama and fresh appeal of when you were sitting around the kitchen table as a young child listening to it being told by your great uncle Harvey.

If you want to write a memoir or life story, just gather as many of the individual stories as you can remember and then bridge them together into a flowing, coherent narrative.

Tales and Fables

This genre is usually passed down through the generations by word of mouth. However, it is becoming more and more common to get the tale in the original dialect down on tape or paper in order to make sure that the heritage, culture, and wisdom are not lost. By using a tape recorder or video it is possible to capture the sound of a particular accent, which is valuable. Video also allows you to gather the body language which is more believable and understanding than the verbal communications.

Authors note: When I wrote my mother's life story, my siblings insisted that I include the favorite family fairy tale, which was told in the car when traveling. It is called "One Eye, Two Eyes and Three Eyes" and I think my grandmother must have made it up because I have never seen it in print anywhere. On a long road trip recently, while I was telling the story in order to lure the grandchildren into a nap, our adult daughter became incensed that I was trying to change the "voice" of the wicked stepsister. She insisted that it had always been much higher and squeakier when Grandma told it!

Tributes

Tributes are similar to eulogies except they are written and spoken about a living person and may contain many more

personal stories than would be shared with a large group.

They are usually a way to show someone how much he/she means to us and how they have touched our lives. Often people will include a short tribute on the bottom of a greeting card.

A tribute is sometimes used as a gift or keepsake for a funeral, anniversary, milestone birthday, retirement or special occasion.

Friends, relatives, co-workers and other interested people are asked to record memories of the one being honored. This may be handled by sending out simple forms to invited guests or interested parties to be filled out and either returned at the occasion or mailed in earlier so that a "Book of Remembrance" can be made.

Can you think of other written life narratives that you have access to? How about backs of photos? A person never really dies as long as there are those who remember them. Every time we find a little clue or remembrance of someone, our hearts and minds are filled with their spirit.

Do your great grandchildren a favor and leave them a written legacy of love. Start on your life story today.

Does it matter which method you use to record your life story? No! You may choose several methods to make your mark on history.

What does matter is that you do something, whether it is to expand on a project already started, or to begin today to record bits and pieces. Your story is unique and the lessons that you have to share are valuable.

The written word creates a legacy that will live through many generations. The act of writing a message, no matter how long, verbose, and detailed, or short, sweet, and off-the-cuff, is a priceless gift.

This gift benefits both the storyteller and the reader.

Reasons for Recording Your Life Story

1. No one else will do it for you.

2. No one else knows the stories of your life quite like you do. Do you want them to tell it?

3. This is an opportunity to share knowledge, wisdom and advice to those who would be inspired to learn from us.

4. When we record something, we remember more.

5. By reflection and recording we are able to gain a deeper appreciation for all the surrounding happenings that influenced our decisions and experiences.

6. A life examined and recorded is twice precious—first the experience itself and then the memories it evokes when we read about it later.

7. Everyone has a story to tell. We each have a unique view of history from our own perspective.

8. There is an inner need in each of us to be remembered- to reflect and to see that our lives had value.

9. We want to be remembered by descendants as a real person and not just a name on a tree.

10. If not recorded, the stories you learned from your grandparents will die with you.

11. The things you did as a child are as remote from children today as the sun is from the earth.

12. You will be looking at painful memories of childhood with the eyes of an adult and realize that they no longer have the power to hurt you.

13. You have the opportunity to leave a legacy for friends and family.

14. This is a way to celebrate your own life.

15. It allows family and friends to know you as an individual, not just the role they were familiar with.

16. By sharing how you overcame adversity, you may strengthen another who is facing a hard time.

17. It gives you an opportunity to examine not only events, but feelings and emotions.

18. It allows you the opportunity to say on paper what is sometimes hard to express in person.

19. By writing our stories, we can examine our life's journey with a wider view.

20. It is very therapeutic and healing to examine the past and release the old hurts.

21. It is the ultimate journey of self-discovery, even if no one else ever reads it.

22. You can pass down traditions, standards, beliefs, or even recipes that have a great deal of meaning within the family or community.

23. As you grow older and less verbal, it helps caregivers and others to see you as you once were.

24. You will be respected, envied, and praised for doing what most people just talk about doing.

And finally............

25. A recent survey taken of a group of elderly people indicated that their major life regrets were in not:

> **Taking more risks.** They choose the secure over the unknown and the unknown would have been fine.
>
> **Reflecting more.** They regretted not taking time to stop along the way and decide who they were and where they were going.
>
> **Contributing more.** They regretted not sharing more feelings, thoughts, time, money and emotions with family, friends and community.

Author's note: By recording your life story, which is a scary step to take, you can accomplish all three.

There is an old African saying that every time a person dies, it is as if a library has burned down.

Write your story today!

Write Your Slice of Life - 6 Easy Steps

Do you know why the "Chicken Soup for the Soul" series is so popular? Aside from terrific marketing and unequaled publicity, readers love the stories and personal essays. They are short, personal and teach a lesson or moral. If you would like to be a better writer of the personal essay, opinion pieces, reports and letters to the editor just follow the suggestions listed below:

1. Be brief.

Many written reports or stories are 500 words or less. However, there is a general rule that an essay is between two and twenty typed, double-spaced pages. The most important criteria to remember is that a good piece needs to be an unbroken reading experience. The reader will lose interest if it is too long or wordy.

2. Tell a story.

A personal essay is a story that has happened to you or that you know about firsthand. The reader assumes that it is nonfiction and that it will contain details and descriptions with which we are familiar. Structure your story around examples, using a pencil as your paintbrush to evoke images and paint a picture in the reader's mind.

3. Make a point.

You will want to illustrate your point, teach a lesson, explain a specific topic, or even support or criticize an idea. Your goal is to win sympathy or agreement. Do not turn it into a sermon or a soapbox to present the superiority of your ideas by including "shoulds" or "musts" aimed at the reader.

4. Use your senses.

Enliven your essay with sensuous detail like how it smelled, tasted, sounded or felt. Make the reader feel like they are seeing and experiencing it through your body.

5. Tell about the ordinary.

Personal essays are often best when they describe a common but freely shared experience. It doesn't have to be about being a survivor of the Twin Towers. Talk about your reaction to 911. Or tell us about watching a sunset or baking bread. When you talk about walking your dog, take us along.

6. Make it engaging.

An essay should arouse curiosity about life. Instead of preaching, invite us to consider your point of view by sharing the particular experience that brought you there, describe what happened, how you reacted, and why you interpret your experiences the way you do.

Think about your own interests and areas of special knowledge, activities, skills, attitudes, problems as well as typical obstacles faced in life. Teach us what you gained or lost in your life lesson. It is much easier to be convincing when you can draw from personal and firsthand information.

Write it today. Submit it to Chicken Soup for the Soul or your local newspaper and become a published author. There are readers out there who want to **share your slice of life.**

About The Author

Who is Judy H. Wright *aka Auntie Artichoke?*

& What's with the Artichoke?

Judy is a parent educator, family coach, and personal historian who has written more than 20 books, hundreds of articles and speaks internationally on family issues, including care giving. Trained as a ready to learn consultant, she works with Head Start organizations and child care resource centers. She also volunteers time writing end-of-life stories for Hospice.

She and Dwain, her husband of 40 years, have six grown children and seven grandchildren. They consider their greatest success in life that their children like themselves and each other. The honorary title of "Auntie" is given in many cultures to the wise women who guide and mentor others in life.

The artichoke also became a teaching lesson when Judy, with her young family, moved into military housing in California to find Artichokes in their yard. Given that it takes two years for the vegetable to flower, the original gardener never got to see the seeds of her labor. Many times, our actions and reactions in life are felt by people we will never meet, but we plant the seeds of kindness anyway.

The symbol of the artichoke has great meaning in her teaching and writing. As she works with families, she sees frequently only the outer edges are exposed and can be prickly, hard to open and sometimes bitter to the taste. They are closed to new ideas or methods. Many families prefer the known over the unknown, even when the old patterns and skills are not serving them well.

But as you expose the artichoke and people to warmth, caring, and time, gradually the leaves begin to open and expose the real treasure—the heart.

You will enjoy Judy's approachable manner, wonderful storytelling and common-sense solutions gleaned from working with hundreds of families and organizations just like yours. Your encounter with Judy will leave you feeling inspired, entertained and especially motivated. Visit Judy's website for excellent references and a full listing of books, workshop topics, tele-classes and testimonials.

To make arrangements for your group or organization to enjoy having Judy present a keynote address, workshop or training session, please contact her at:

Judy H. Wright aka Auntie Artichoke,

the Storytelling Trainer

(406) 549-9813,

Email: Judy@ArtichokePress.com

www.ArtichokePress.com

"Finding the heart of the story in the journey of life."

Free eBook at www.UseEncouragingWords.com

"Visiting with Judy is like having a cup of tea with a loving auntie."
"We are all grateful for the incredible work you do to birth these stories."

Resources for Parents, Teachers and other Caring Adults

http://www.ArticlesbyJudy.com Free articles on relationships/parenting/grief/personal development Free to use in your blog-just keep content and contact info intact.

http://www.JudyHWright.com Personal website for Judy H. Wright, including blog and articles. Connect with Judy for empowerment coaching and inspirational speaking engagements.

http://www.ArtichokePress.com Main website for Judy H Wright, full listing of books, workshops, radio shows, tele-classes. Free report available.

http://www.BounceBackPerson.com Site for Judy's latest book, *Out Of Balance? Be a Bounce Back Person*. Includes bonus items.

http://www.EmpowermentWithJudy.com Mentoring and MasterMind. Not empowerment for Judy or by Judy, but with Judy. Walking life's journey together.

http://www.KidsChoresandMore.com Site for Judy's book, *Kids, Chores, And More*. Includes bonus items. Free report available.

http://www.TheLeftOutChild.com Site for the importance of friendship, Sign up for our free e-course

http://www.AskAuntieArtichoke.com Blog for parenting and relationships. Please leave comments and questions. You will be glad you did.

http://www.IfDeathIsNear.com Blog for those facing the loss of a loved one.

http://www.DeathOfMyPet.com Book and bonus items for someone who has lost a beloved pet.. Excellent stories and resources for pet lovers.

http://www.CyberbullyingHelp.com Main site for bullying and cyberbullying assistance. Free report and connections to other blogs and websites. Leave comments and share your story.

http://www.UseEncouragingWords.com Main site for free e-book on the power of words and communication.

http://www.DisciplineYesPunishNo.com Site for alternatives to punishment. Transform and strengthen your family connections and communications.

http://www.WelcomeAbundance.com Methods of earning passive streams of income.

http://www.EncourageSelfConfidence.com Site for Judy's book, *Using Encouraging Words to Motivate Positive Action* and bonus items about building self-confidence with encouraging words.

http://www.4LifeHappyKids.com/Judy Goal setting and teaching your children the Law of Attraction.

http://www.JudyHWright.com/GiggleBaby Giggle Baby – Find great clothes and creative products for your children

Thank you for joining our community of kind, thoughtful people who want to model and teach kindness, tolerance and respect for all.

Printed in Great Britain
by Amazon

61583342R00031